Praying in the Key of 'C'
Book II
With Devotional Journal

©2009 by Patty Harris
ISBN1 978-1-931314-11-4
All rights reserved. No part of this book may be reproduced in any manner whatsoever without the written permission of the Author and Publisher. All scripture references are from the King James Version of the Holy Bible. Published by Olive Press Publishing an imprint of Grief Relief Publishing Co,

*The Body of Christ must remain in
the sacred place of prayer.
We must be intentional about maturing our prayer
life through an intimate relationship with God
through Jesus Christ.*
Patty Harris

~

*Prayer does not equip us for greater work –
Prayer is the greater work.*
Oswald Chambers

Day 1 — First Things First — Genesis 1:1a

In the Beginning God...

The first four words of the Holy Bible declares *"In the beginning God..."* Everything else flows from this! To develop as intercessors, we must not only believe in the God of the Bible, we must believe God!

Hebrews 11:6 tells us *But without faith it is impossible to please him: for he that cometh to God must believe that He is, and that He is a rewarder of them that diligently seek Him.*

Cometh to in the Greek means *to approach; to draw near spiritually*. On this journey of growing, maturing, and developing in our relationship with God we must believe that God is! Believe that God is who He says He is and that He will perform that which He says He will perform.

Exercising our faith is the key to communication with God. When we come before God in prayer, we must come in faith believing that God is a rewarder of them that diligently seek Him.

The believers' prayer life and relationship with God cannot and will not develop on its own. If left alone, a healthy prayer life and relationship with God will cease to exist with power and authority. If this happens, many promises of God to the believer will not come to pass. Prayer is the birth canal for the promises of God to be born or made manifest in the earth.

It is in prayer that we must seek the face of God not just the hand of God. In seeking God's face, we desire to become like Him in character that the life and love of Jesus Christ can be seen in and through each believer. In seeking the hand of God, we are only praying for what we can get from God. We only pray for God's blessings, material things, and promises. Be careful to not seek 'things' from God and not seek after His character in our hearts. When we seek first the Promisor the promises will be manifest.

Believe that God is faithful to his word. If we draw near to Him, He will draw near to us. God is the same yesterday, today, and forevermore!!!

Notes:

Day 2   The Power of Prayer   Luke 1:37

For with God nothing shall be impossible.

    All the possibilities in God come through prayer. Prayer is a personal invitation from God to be involved in His activity on earth. God not only invites us to call on Him - God expects us to pray. All Christians are called to pray. No one in the body of Christ can stand before the Lord and say they didn't have anything to do. Only some are called to be apostles, some are called to be prophets, some are called to be evangelists, some are called to be pastors, and teachers. However, all are called to be pray-ers!!!

    Prayer is far reaching in its influence and effects. Through answered prayer Moses saved a nation; Hannah conceived her son Samuel; Samuel brought revival; Jesus brought Lazarus back from the dead; Jesus fed thousands; Hezekiah's health was restored. So much has been accomplished because of the power of prayer.

    Prayer to God reaches from across the street to across international borders. It travels through time zones. Prayer goes everywhere and so does God's answer.

    The target of prayer is the ear of God. Therefore, there must be oneness with Christ. We cannot treat our prayer life casually. Like worship, prayer must become our lifestyle. We can talk about all the awesome answered prayers that are in the Bible, however, there should be a little spiritual jealousy. Jesus Christ has promised that we can do even more because He has gone to the Father. The Church, the Body of Christ should be experiencing more answered prayer than is recorded in the Bible because of Jesus Christ in us. Since prayer is a partnership with God, God desires for someone with His heart to plead *"Thy will be done ... "* When we ask, God can act! Let us experience impossibilities through answered prayer.

Notes:

Day 3   You Are God's Representative   John 20:21

Then said Jesus to them again, Peace be unto you: as my Father hath sent Me, even so send I you.

This word *send* means to *send forth on a certain mission or to take care of business.* The one sent is an ambassador or representative of the one sending.

God has always declared the necessity of mankind. This is manifested in His Son Jesus Christ coming to earth as God's Word made flesh. Jesus came to fulfill the Father's will and not to do His own. God needed Jesus on earth to fulfill His will. God sent Jesus into the world as the Word made flesh to fulfill His plan of redemption. Jesus had the authority of the Father with Him. We find in this scripture that Jesus sent forth His disciples as ambassadors or representatives to continue His work. According to II Corinthians 5: 18, Christians have now been entrusted with the ministry of reconciliation. Jesus sends us forth to represent Him in the earth. To represent means to *re-present.* We are to re-present Jesus Christ in the earth. As His disciples we are here in His stead. Actually it is Christ in us continuing to reach out to humanity with a message of salvation. He can only minister through us as we are yielded to and walk in obedience to Him.

The Lord Jesus not only sends us forth as His disciples, He releases within us the same power and fullness of the Holy Spirit which He had while on earth. If we are fulfilling His purpose we will have His power! Just as prayer kept Jesus connected to the Father we must pray and remain connected. If we are not in constant connection with the Father we can't continue His work - only ours. We must have the same mind-set as Jesus Christ if we are to accomplish God's will on the earth. We must work with God not apart from God. God acknowledges His dependence on us as vessels through which He can exert His power in the earth.

Notes:

Day 4   Why God Needs You to Pray   Isaiah 59:16

And He saw that there was no man, and wondered that there was no intercessor: therefore his arm brought salvation unto Him; and his righteousness, it sustained him.

This word *wondered* is the Hebrew word *shamem*. It means *to grow numb; to devastate; to stun and stupefy*. It is something so horrible that it leaves a person speechless. Shamem is also the word that is used to describe Tamar after she was raped by her brother in II Samuel 13:20.

We find in this scripture that God was actually devastated that there was no one praying or interceding. Can you imagine God being speechless because His people do not pray?

God has entrusted so much to and through the Church and the Christian through the power of prayer. It is a devastating thing before God when people do not pray. Prayer is our divine connection for transacting God's business here on earth. God has chosen to respond to and answer prayer. Answered prayer is God's idea!!!

God has always chosen to work through mankind, not around mankind and not without mankind. When the children of Israel needed to be delivered God accomplished it through Moses. When salvation was needed, God sent His only begotten Son in the form of a man to save and redeem mankind from the curse of the enemy. There is something that God desires to fulfill in the earth through you. There is someone whose life God wants to touch through you. You praying for someone else could be their answer!

With all that is happening in the world today – the Body of Christ needs to return to prayer! There is much power released when we pray. Some things will not turn around any other way – except we pray. People are transgressing against the laws of God as never before. We need to pray and ask God to turn nations back to Him. May God give the Body of Christ a praying spirit.

Notes:

Day 5 — When Jesus Prayed — John 11:38-44

Jesus therefore again groaning in himself cometh to the grave. It was a cave, and a stone lay upon it. 39 Jesus said, Take ye away the stone. Martha, the sister of him that was dead, saith unto him, Lord, by this time he stinketh: for he hath been dead four days. 40 Jesus saith unto her, Said I not unto thee, that, if thou wouldest believe, thou shouldest see the glory of God? 41 Then they took away the stone from the place where the dead was laid. And Jesus lifted up his eyes, and said, Father, I thank thee that thou hast heard me. 42 And I knew that thou hearest me always: but because of the people which stand by I said it, that they may believe that thou hast sent me. 43 And when he thus had spoken, he cried with a loud voice, Lazarus, come forth. 44 And he that was dead came forth, bound hand and foot with graveclothes: and his face was bound about with a napkin. Jesus saith unto them, Loose him, and let him go.

When Jesus prayed things happened. As we examine the life of the Lord Jesus Christ, we find that while on earth, Jesus was a man of prayer! In fact, it seemed to be the center of His life. Jesus often withdrew from the crowds to be alone with the Father in prayer.

The gospels remind us that the signs and wonders that Jesus performed were all preceded with prayer.

~ Before Jesus called Lazarus out of the grave - He prayed!
~ Before feeding five thousand - Jesus prayed!
~ Immediately after His baptism - Jesus prayed!
~ Prior to selecting the twelve disciples - Jesus prayed!
~ Intensive prayer preceded His battle with the enemy!
~ The night before His crucifixion, not only did Jesus pray for the disciples, He struggled in prayer as He faced betrayal and death!
~ Jesus prayed on the cross!
~ Jesus prayed the prayer of victory!
~ Jesus is seated at the right hand of the Father - interceding for us!

To be like Jesus, we must pray! Without praying we cannot fully embrace *the all of who we are in Christ!* Because he had a relationship with the Father, when Jesus prayed - things happened. God answered! God will do the same for us today as we pray in faith and believe God.

Like Jesus, we must make time to be alone with the Father. Alone in His presence!

Notes:

Day 6   Let the Word become Flesh   John 1:14

And the Word was made flesh, and dwelt among us, (and we beheld His glory, the glory as of the only begotten of the Father) full of grace and truth.

God gave His Word a body - and made His Word flesh. His promises to heal, deliver, love, and forgive took on human form. God then gave His Word made flesh a name. Jesus! God also desires to continue to give His Word a body – the Church. Not just a building made of brick and mortar, but each believer should house the Word of the Lord within.

As we read, pray, meditate on, and walk in obedience to the Word of God, He will become our nature. The Word will begin to take on flesh. We become grafted into Christ and His Word becomes grafted into us.

The Word will become our influence in life's decisions. It will shape our thoughts, desires, and even form our words. This is done through time spent with God. We must ask God to help us to apply His Word to our daily life then walk in obedience to that Word. This is how the Word becomes flesh.

This is how we become doers of the Word and not hearers only. Many people know what the Word says, however, struggle to walk in obedience to it.

Matthew 5: 16 reminds us to *Let your light so shine before men, that they may see your good works, and glorify your Father which is in heaven.* We are also to be a light. What does a light do? It dispels darkness. The Word made flesh did not invite darkness by using negative language and ungodly conduct. Do you dispel or invite darkness by your conduct and your speech?

Notes:

Day 7   Come Clean Before God   Psalms 51:3, 10

For I acknowledge my transgressions: and my sin is ever before me, 10 Create in me a clean heart, O God, and renew a right spirit within me.

   David had committed sins against God in that he committed adultery with Bathsheba then had her husband Uriah killed. David confessed his sin to God and asked God to restore him. Read through Psalms 51 and see how David prayed to God. He also asked God to not take His Spirit from Him. This is powerful.

   When we know the power of God's Spirit and anointing within us, we should guard that and not allow sin to rob us of the best God has invested within us. Sin robs us of all that God has for us. Psalms 66:18 firmly tells us *If I regard iniquity in my heart, the Lord will not hear me.* To *regard* means *to give attention to; to have a firm fixed look.* If we are attending to or living in habitual sin, a life of sin that is clear in scripture violates the lifestyle, character, and conduct of a Christian and don't ask God to forgive and cleanse us, we are separating ourselves from a right relationship with God. We must come clean and confess sin to God and be cleansed from all unrighteousness. God does not have a problem with our sin. He has made provision through His Word to cleanse us from sin. God does have a problem with our lack of confession of sin and choosing to rebel against His Word and live in sin.

   We cannot neglect to confess our sin to God and repent. I John 1:9 lovingly reminds us *If we confess our sins, he is faithful and just to forgive us our sins, and to cleanse us from all unrighteousness.* Only Christ can cleanse us from sin and its power to destroy us. Sin creates a barrier which severs our relationship with God. Only faith in the atoning work of Jesus Christ at Calvary through the shedding of His blood can cleanse us from sin and its power to destroy us. The enemy comes to steal, kill, and destroy. When we are cleansed by the blood of Jesus, the enemy cannot destroy us.

Notes:

Day 8   Clothe Yourself in Christ   Romans 13:14

But put ye on the Lord Jesus Christ, and make not provision for the flesh, to fulfil the lusts thereof.

To *put on* or *to be clothed with a person* is a Greek phrase signifying *to take upon oneself the interests of another; to enter into another persons' views and be wholly and totally on that person's side, imitating them in all things.*

To *put on* a person means *to copy or become like that person.* To profess salvation through Jesus Christ is to take on the life and works of Jesus Christ, follow in His footsteps, and do His works. How do we put on Christ? We must be crucified. Galatians 2:20 tells us *I am crucified with Christ: nevertheless I live; yet not I, but Christ liveth in me: and the life which I now live in the flesh I live by the faith of the Son of God, who loved me, and gave himself for me.* The only way to put on Christ is to crucify self and allow Christ to live in and through you. We must obey His Word. In crucifying self, we take on the character, conduct, and mind set of the Lord Jesus Christ.

We can do this by:
~ Reading the Word of God
~ Meditating on the Word of God - Psalms 1:2
~ Hearing the Word of God - Romans 10:17
~ Live in obedience to the Word - James 1:22

These disciplines allow the Word of God to become flesh with us. We must take on His thoughts and mindset. This is also how we can sustain and maintain the character and conduct of Christ in our daily life. As Christians we must allow the character of Christ to be formed within us. Then in our daily activities of life including our interaction with others, it will be our nature to show forth the character of God because we have *put on Christ.*

Notes:

Day 9 — Forgive — Mark 11:25

And when ye stand praying, forgive, if ye have ought against any: that your Father also which is in heaven may forgive you your trespasses.

This *word forgive* means *to omit; to pardon; bear no malice; to give up resentment against or the desire to punish.* Forgiving the person does not mean you act like nothing happened and disregard them. In forgiving, you give up the bitterness and often the anger that comes to us when someone does us wrong. To forgive sin is to remove the sin from another.

Forgiving another of their sin is not what God is requiring of us. Only God can forgive sin. When God forgives us of our sins, He liberates us from the hold, power, and guilt of sin. We must confess our sin to God and ask Him to forgive us and remove them from us. We are to forgive the person for their action of sinning against us. We sometimes think that if we forgive someone it means they won't sin against us again. This is not always true. If a person speaks lies about you and you forgive them for speaking the lies it is possible that they may lie again. This could be because the person is a liar! It is the persons' character and nature to lie.

There is nothing you can do about this. They must go to God in repentance and ask God to cleanse them from this unrighteousness of being a liar. If we do not forgive, we will soon find that we are consumed with negative thoughts against the individual(s) who harmed us. Not forgiving is like you drinking poison and expecting the other person to get sick.

Forgiveness is one of the ultimate indicators of the indwelling presence of God's Spirit. When we forgive, we are reaching out to others as Christ reached out and continues to reach out to us. We must rely on God's love, protection, promises, grace, mercy, comfort, and healing balm to soothe us. If you find it difficult to forgive, ask God to forgive the person through you.

Notes:

Day 10   **Abide in Christ**   John 15:7-8

If ye abide in me, and my words abide in you, ye shall ask what ye will, and it shall be done unto you. 8 Herein is my Father glorified, that ye bear much fruit; so shall ye be my disciples.

To *abide* means *to stay, to dwell, to endure*. We abide in Christ Jesus by diligently reading, meditating, and walking in obedience to the Word of God. As we abide in Him and allow the word of the Lord to abide in us, transformation takes place. The will of God must become our will. This is how we can ask for anything and receive it. Our want has to be consumed by His will.

If we are not asking in harmony with His word, then we are asking amiss - with wrong motives. Imagine what it would be like if everyone immediately received what they wanted. It would be chaotic! People would want someone else's spouse or house; another's ministry or car. People quite often want what doesn't belong to them. When they can't get it - they steal it.

When we are consumed by God's will and desires - God will give us the desires of our heart because our desires are actually His desires fulfilled in and through us. This is the only way God can trust us with such an awesome blank check from heaven which will allow us to ask what we will and it will be given.

Abiding in the Word allows us to die to self. Galatians 2:20 tells us *I am crucified with Christ: nevertheless I live; yet not I, but Christ liveth in me: and the life which I now live in the flesh I live by the faith of the Son of God, who loved me, and gave Himself for me.*

Abiding allows us to develop and mature spiritually. When we abide in the Word, transformation can begin to take place. According to John 8:31-32, there is a great benefit to abiding in the Word! 31 *Then Jesus said to the Jews who had faith in him, If you keep my word, then you are truly my disciples; 32 And you will have knowledge of what is true, and that will make you free.* (Bible in Basic English).

The truth of the Word of God will set us free. Free from what? Free from any thing, situation, or person that hinders our growth in Christ.

Notes:

Day 11   Have Time Alone with God   I Corinthians 1:9

God is faithful, by whom ye were called unto the fellowship of his Son Jesus Christ our Lord.

Every Christian is called to have fellowship with God. Fellowship means *to have companionship; to spend time with*. When we have fellowship with God, communion takes place. Communion is *the exchange of ideas, thoughts, and even feelings*. God desires to share His heart with us and also to hear what is in our heart. It is in His presence that transformation takes place. Here is where God will give us beauty for ashes; the oil of joy for our mourning. Here is where we can be made whole!! Healing can take place.

The enemy doesn't want this to happen - so his best action is a distraction. We are faced with many distractions that will hinder us from praying and spending time alone with God. The only way to keep
from being distracted is to value the importance of daily time with God. When we value something, it will become a priority in life. God desires that we come into His presence and invites us to do so daily. God desires to be with us so much that He has promised to never leave us nor forsake us and has promised to be Omnipresent - everywhere present. God has also invested Himself in us by His Holy Spirit. When we come into His presence - we don't need to bring a grocery list of requests. Sometimes we need to simply be with God. Take time to listen. Psalms 46:10 encourages us to *Be still, and know that I am God!*

The Hebrew word for *still* in this scripture is *rapa* which means *to loosen; to withdraw; to let someone go*. The basic idea of rapa is *that of relaxing the hands*. Rapa comes from the word *rapha*. Jehovah-Rapha is one of the title names of God which means *God is our healer*. Rapha means *to mend; to make whole; to heal*. When we come into His presence and simply be still, loosen your grip on everyday cares and be in God's presence - God can heal us and make us whole.

Notes:

Day 12   Meditate the Word of God   Joshua 1:8

This book of the law shall not depart out of thy mouth; but thou shalt meditate therein day and night, that thou mayest observe to do according to all that is written therein: for then thou shalt make thy way prosperous, and then thou shalt have good success.

This word *meditate* is *hagah* and means *to speak, to mutter, to whisper.* It describes the low moaning sound like that of a dove. Meditation has a purpose. God told Joshua to meditate. Why? So that Joshua would be able to do everything that he had meditated on. Then came the promise from God that *you will be prosperous and successful.* Prosperity and success follows meditating the Word and walking in obedience to the Word you've been meditating.

Many people think they don't know how to meditate. Do you know how to worry??? If so, then you can meditate. Worry is simply speaking and reviewing a problem over and over again. Worry is negative meditation which makes us feel worse. Instead of reviewing and speaking the problem, review and speak the answer which is the Word of God.

Meditating on the Word of God helps to renew our mind. It allows us to marinate in the Word and the Word can have a chance to saturate into us so that the Holy Spirit can transform our thinking. It allows the Word to be made flesh. God's Word is always speaking to us. Even when we close the Bible, the Word is still alive - talking to us, convicting us, teaching us and guiding us. We must obey when the Word speaks! Then we will make our way prosperous.

To start a time of meditation, simply find a quiet place where you can concentrate. Read a small portion of scripture. You can even write it down. Read and speak it aloud to yourself. You need to hear yourself speak the Word of God. This helps memorize the Word. There should be a response to the Word. Is this Word calling you to repent; to worship; to forgive? What is the Holy Spirit prompting in your spirit? Write it down. End your time with praise.

Notes:

Day 13   Let the Praise Begin   Psalms 150:6

Let everything that hath breath praise the LORD. Praise ye the LORD.

Praise is always *what's happening in heaven!* Revelation 5: 11- 14 tells us *And I beheld, and I heard the voice of many angels round about the throne and the beasts and the elders: and the number of them was ten thousand times ten thousand, and thousands of thousands; 11 Saying with a loud voice, Worthy is the Lamb that was slain to receive power, and riches, and wisdom, and strength, and honour, and glory, and blessing.*

If you want the surround sound of heaven to invade your space, your home, even your innermost being - begin to join with the angels and praise God! This is the atmosphere where God dwells. Psalms 22:3 tells us *But thou art holy, O thou that inhabits the praises of Israel.* This word *inhabit* in the Hebrew is *yashab* and it means *to sit down, to settle in, to marry, to remain, to abide.* God loves to be where He is being praised - and He stays there! Where the presence of the Lord is the enemy cannot stay.

Praise will change the atmosphere from one of despair to one of victory. Psalms 100:4 lets us know that praise is the gateway to God. We are told to *Enter into his gates with thanksgiving, and into his courts with praise: be thankful unto him, and bless his name.* It isn't difficult to connect with or communicate with God. As born again believers, the Spirit of God dwells within us. We are reminded in I Corinthians 6:19-20 that our body is the temple of the Holy Spirit. Because of this intimate relationship we can pray and praise God at any time in any situation and in any place – and God will meet us where we are.

We do not have to wait for a Sunday service to communicate with God and experience the refreshing in our soul that comes from being in His presence. Begin to praise God! When the enemy tries to bring heaviness and doubt begin to praise God for being Who He IS!!! You are never alone when praising God. You are joining with the angels and the host of heaven.

Notes:

Day 14   Be Holy even as God is Holy   I Peter 1:15-16

But as he which hath called you is holy, so be ye holy in all manner of conversation; 16 Because it is written, Be ye holy; for I am holy.

The basic idea of *holy* is *to be consecrated; to be devoted to God; to share in God's purity and abstain from earth's defilements.* The significance of holiness is moral not ritual. It flows from within because of the Holy Spirit. As Christians, we must have the mind of Christ. The character of Christ must be our character.

Conduct is *what we do, our outward life.* Character is *who we are, the unseen life.* Although it is hidden, our character is evidenced by our conduct. Character is the state of the heart while conduct is the outward expression.

The enemy tries to govern our thoughts and affect our character and conduct. If he can get us thinking his thoughts, he will succeed in getting our character and conduct to be contrary to the Word of God.

We must be careful to guard against "looking" holy by our conduct and not allowing holiness to flow from the heart. Jesus had this problem with the Pharisees. We find that in the teachings of Jesus Christ, He is concerned about our inward spiritual character and integrity not just the outward appearance. In Matthew 23:28, Jesus tells the Pharisees *Even so ye also outwardly appear righteous unto men, but within ye are full of hypocrisy and iniquity.*

The atoning work of Jesus Christ is to create Godly character and conduct within the Christian, *Who gave himself for us, so that he might make us free from all wrongdoing, and make for himself a people clean in heart and on fire with good works* (Titus 2:14 - Bible in Basic English).

Jesus has provided Himself as our way of holiness, He will cleanse and create within us a new heart and teach us how to walk in holiness - if we ask Him!! !

Notes:

Day 15   Pray Without Ceasing   I Thess. 5:17

Pray without ceasing.

Ceasing means *uninterruptedly,* i.e. *without omission.* Because of the indwelling presence of the Holy Spirit, believers have a "constant connection" to God. We have a direct line to God and God has a direct line to us. This is what fellowship is about. We should talk to God and share every area of our life with God: our concerns, sorrows, challenges, joys, triumphs, everything. Our mindset should always be in a mode to share with God,

Reasons to pray are all around us. Some of the televised news events are reasons to pray; the Holy Spirit may bring someone to our mind, a face or a name; a church, or even nations. If we see an auto accident or an ambulance, this is reason to pray for others. This is also how God prompts us to pray - when we see these situations happening, bring it before the Lord. In doing this we are also cultivating an awareness of the presence of God.

In every situation in life, prayer should be the most natural response and outpouring of the heart before God. Our heart must always be filled with the spirit of prayer and always ready to meet with God. To pray without ceasing reminds us that prayer requires a relationship with God. This verse does not mean that we are to do nothing except pray - unless this is the life that God has called you to!

We read in Luke 2:36-37 of Anna, the prophetess who lived in the temple and prayed day and night. It does, however mean that we must never lose our awareness of our relationship and attention to pray and to the Lord. Our prayer life should be intertwined with our daily life, We should always be a constant connection to God,

Notes:

Day 16   Pray According to God's Will   I John 5:14

And this is the confidence that we have in him, that, if we ask any thing according to his will, he heareth us…

Our confidence in God answering our prayers is based on asking according to or in harmony with His Will which is His Word. We come to know and understand God's will through reading God's Word. God and His Word are one.

When we read, meditate, and study the Word of God, the Holy Spirit will also reveal to us principles that are applicable to the situations we face in life. There are some things that we already know are the will of God which can be prayed. It is always the will of God that:

1. All persons come to repentance and faith in Jesus Christ.
   II Peter 3:9; I Timothy 2:4
2. The world be evangelized. Matthew 28:19; 24:14
3. Christians grow in Christlikeness. Ephesians 4: 13, 15

Facts about God's will for the Christian to observe:
1. We should seek it as Jesus did - John 5:30
2. We should seek to understand it - Ephesians 5: 17
3. We should perform it from the heart - Ephesians 6:6
4. We should make performing it our will- John 4:34
5. It establishes our relationship with Jesus Christ – Matthew 15:20

Notes:

Day 17　　　　　　Pray God's Word　　　　　Psalms 119:89

For ever, O LORD, thy word is settled in heaven.

Prayer should draw its life from the Word of God. Praying the Word of God will bring results and answers. Isaiah 55:11 tells us that God's Word *'will not return unto Him void.* This means it will not lie. God's Word will not return to God without accomplishing what God sent it out to fulfill.

We must remember that we are not to simply pray God's Word just for the sake of having a religious activity. When the Word of God mixes with faith, the Holy Spirit can release power through our life and prayers. We must value and honor the Word of God because it holds within it the answer to every situation we will encounter in life. God will meet us where we are with the faith that we have in His Word.

Praying the Word

When praying the scriptures, change pronouns to personal ones such as he, she, they or I. It is not unscriptural to pray with your eyes open as you read God's Word. You may often find that applying the scriptures to your personal life and its situations will allow God to reveal His will for you. Be sensitive to the leading of the Holy Spirit as you pray God's word.

Reasons to pray the Word

1. It allows us to pray very specific prayers.
2. The Word of God gives us a prayer vocabulary that is directly from the Lord which gives us confidence and boldness to defeat the enemy.
3. The Word of God allows us to pray with power.
4. Scripture praying, especially from the Psalms can express our own condition, thoughts, attitudes, and emotions. Many scriptures can be used as a launching point for requests in prayer. Some scriptures are already in personal form and can be prayed such as: Psalms 27; Psalms 91. The Psalms are a good place to start.

Notes:

Day 18   Praying When We Don't Know God's Will

II Timothy 3:16

All scripture is given by inspiration of God, and is profitable for doctrine, for reproof, for correction, for instruction in righteousness

We can always pray regarding those aspects of God's will that we know to be appropriate to the situation. If someone is unsaved, we know to pray for his/her salvation because it is God's will that all men be saved. However, there are times when we are unsure regarding God's divine plan for a specific situation.

When we don't fully understand the will of God in a situation, it requires patient resting in the Lord and confident trust that God's answer will be revealed. It is in times like these that we become vulnerable to the attacks of the enemy. We must guard our heart from becoming discouraged and disheartened. This will causes our faith to waver.

This will also cause us to become anxious. We must ask God to release within us His peace and willingness to accept His answer. We may not yet be ready to accept the will of God. Here is where in the midst of praying it becomes a struggle to not only know God's will but to accept God's it. Even Jesus experienced this in the garden of Gethsemane when He said, *"nevertheless, not My will, but Thine be done ... "* Even though Jesus knew what the perfect will of the Father was, there was still at that moment in His humanity a struggle in accepting the will of God. There are many aspects of God's will that can become topics of bold prayer.

James 1:5 - Pray for wisdom. When we don't know God's will, ask God for wisdom. Scripture assures us that God desires to answer our prayer for wisdom.

James 1:2-4 - In the midst of tribulation, we can pray that the difficult circumstances will bring about spiritual growth. We see from this scripture that God does intend for spiritual growth to come out of trials. This spiritual truth can form the basis for praying that God will produce growth in us or others.

Notes:

Day 19 Pray to the Father in the Name of Jesus John 16:23

And in that day ye shall ask me nothing. Verily, verily, I say unto you, Whatsoever ye shall ask the Father in my name, he will give it you.

We are to pray to the Father in the name of Jesus. Our access to God is through Jesus Christ. Scripture reminds us that there is one mediator between God and man and that is Christ Jesus. *For there is one God, and one mediator between God and men, the man Christ Jesus.* I Timothy 2:5.

Jesus tells us to ask of the Father in His name. The word *name* in scripture is *onoma*. Onoma indicates *character and authority*. What we ask for in prayer must be in line with the character of Jesus Christ. If it is not in line with His character, it is not in line with His will. If it is not in line with God's will, God's power cannot enforce it. Asking is not limited to salvation. Jesus has promised that we could ask for *"whatsoever," "anything,"* and *"all things"* in His name and it would be granted. However, it must be done in and through His name.

Here are a few things Scripture tells us we can ask for:

I. **Holy Spirit**- Luke 11:11-13
If a son shall ask bread of any of you that is a father, will he give him a stone? or if he ask a fish, will he for a fish give him a serpent? 12 Or if he shall ask an egg, will he offer him a scorpion? 13 If ye then, being evil, know how to give good gifts unto your children: how much more shall your heavenly Father give the Holy Spirit to them that ask him?

2. **Wisdom** - James 1:5-7
If any of you lack wisdom, let him ask of God, that giveth to all men liberally, and upbraideth not; and it shall be given him. 6 But let him ask in faith, nothing wavering. For he that wavereth is like a wave of the sea driven with the wind and tossed. 7 For let not that man think that he shall receive any thing of the Lord.

3. **Good things** - Matthew 7:11
If ye then, being evil, know how to give good gifts unto your children, how much more shall your Father which is in heaven give good things to them that ask him?

Notes:

Day 20   Seek the Lord   Matthew 6:33

But seek ye first the kingdom of God, and his righteousness; and all these things shall be added unto you.

    To *seek* means to *search for eagerly*. We are told many times in scripture to *seek the Lord*. Seeking requires effort and tenacity. We seek after something that we desire. It takes discipline, effort, and devotion to seek after the Lord. We are to seek Him – not what He can give us.

    So many blessings await the Christian who will seek the Lord. The treasures of understanding, wisdom, complete joy, true love, and the secret things of the Lord belong to those who will seek Him. It takes discipline, devotion, and effort to seek the face of the Lord. Because seeking requires much effort, the lazy Christian is not willing to seek the face of the Lord - only His hand for what they can get from God without much effort. We must want HIM - not HIS stuff!!

    Colossians 2:3 tells us that all the treasures of wisdom and knowledge are hidden in the Lord. In the book of Colossians Paul pictures the Church as a treasure field. Great treasures are hidden in this field - or the Church. However, this treasure is not material possessions - it is spiritual. Wisdom and knowledge are great treasures of the Kingdom of God that we need and must seek.

Seeking God must be done:

- With the whole heart - Deuteronomy 4:29
- Continually - I Chronicles 16: 11
- Diligently - Hebrews 11:6

We are to seek:

- God's Kingdom first - Luke 12:31
- Things above - Colossians 3: 1
- Blessings of seeking God:
- Life - Psalms 69:22
- Righteousness - Psalms 10: 12
- Rewards - Hebrews 11:6

Notes:

Day 21 **Be Filled with the Holy Spirit** Ephesians 5:18

And be not drunk with wine, wherein is excess; but be filled with the Spirit;

The Holy Spirit lives within those who have come to Christ in repentance and faith. The Holy Spirit is the Spirit of the Lord Jesus Christ who resides within the believer. Without the Holy Spirit true worship to God cannot happen. Without the indwelling Holy Spirit we are helpless to live a righteous life. Our body is the temple of the Holy Spirit. Since the Holy Spirit knows the mind of God, He can enable us to pray according to the will of God and to live righteously. Having the Holy Spirit within does not guarantee that we will always pray right or live right however, it does mean that we can. He releases this power within us.

The Holy Spirit need only be received by faith and not by works. If you have not been filled with the Holy Spirit all you have to do is ask: *God, I ask in the name of Jesus that You would fill me with Your Holy Spirit so that I can pray right and live according to Your Word. In Jesus name, Amen.*

Read the follow scriptures to understand the ministry of the Holy Spirit in the life of the Believer.

The Holy Spirit:
1. Can lead us - Romans 8: 14
2. Dwells only the believer - Romans 8:9
3. Helps in prayer - Romans 8:26-27
4. Knows the things of God - I Corinthians 2: 11
5. Imparts gifts to Believers - 1Corinthians 12: 1-11
6. Makes us free from sin and death - Romans 8: 1-4
7. Helps us obey the truth - I Peter 1:22
8. Is eternal- Hebrews 9:14
9. Imparts the character of God - Galatians 5:22
10. Word of God is the sword of the Spirit - Ephesians 6: 17

Notes:

Day 22   Ask   Matthew 7:11

If ye then, being evil, know how to give good gifts unto your children, how much more shall your Father which is in heaven give good things to them that ask him?

The idea here is to ask for something that is due a child because of family rights. A child has a right to ask for good things from a parent. God invites us to ask of Him as a child asking from a parent. However, it should be done out of a relationship with God not apart from it.

When we are in relationship with God through Christ Jesus we can ask boldly and with confidence. Otherwise, we will only go to God in times of crisis as if God were our personal 'grocery store' to fulfill what is on our list. God desires the best for us and is willing to give it if we would ask in faith.

Here are some things we can ask for:

1. Needs and wants - Matthew 6:8
2. Holy Spirit - Luke 11:9-13
3. Wisdom - James 1:5-8
4. Life - I John 5:16
5. Help from God - II Chronicles 20:4
6. Anything - Matthew 18: 19; John 14: 14;
7. Whatsoever - Matthew 21:22
8. Help of God - II Chronicles 20:4

Notes:

Day 23   **Pray with Thanksgiving**   Philippians 4:6-7

Be careful for nothing; but in every thing by prayer and supplication with thanksgiving let your requests be made known unto God. 7 And the peace of God, which passeth all understanding, shall keep your hearts and minds through Christ Jesus.

This word *careful* in the Greek means *to be anxious about*. When we are anxious we are worried. Any situation that causes concern or worry is a situation that needs to be brought before the Lord in prayer. Worry and/or concern should be an automatic call to prayer.

Thanksgiving is *an active grateful language to God as an act of worship*. When we pray with thanksgiving we are thanking God for the answer and believing that God will settle the situation. Even if we can't see the answer we can believe and give thanks that God will reveal it.

There is an exchange that takes place when we give thanks. It is told to us in verse seven. *The peace of God will keep our hearts and minds through Christ Jesus.* To *keep* means *to guard; protect; to hem in*. What will the peace of God protect? It will protect our minds, hearts, and bodies from the effects of worry which is distress. Some of the effects of distress are inner turmoil, illness, and disease.

Colossians 4:2 reminds us to *continue in prayer, and watch in the same with thanksgiving ...*

Thanksgiving closes the door to doubt and unbelief. When we begin to thank God for the answer we are reminding ourselves that God has each situation in His hands. When we believe that God has each situation in His hands, we can have assurance and peace that God will be faithful to answer our prayer.

Notes:

Day 24   Pray with Importunity   Luke 11:5-8

And he said unto them, Which of you shall have a friend, and shall go unto him at midnight, and say unto him, Friend, lend me three loaves; 6 For a friend of mine in his journey is come to me, and I have nothing to set before him? 7 And he from within shall answer and say, Trouble me not: the door is now shut, and my children are with me in bed; I cannot rise and give thee. 8 I say unto you, Though he will not rise and give him, because he is his friend, yet because of his importunity he will rise and give him as many as he needeth.

   Importunity is *persistence in requesting or demanding; to make urgent and repeated requests or demands; to ask for something urgently or repeatedly.*
   This man made an urgent request on behalf of someone else. This is intercession!!! Intercession means to intercede. To intercede is *to plead or make a request on behalf of another or others; to intervene for the purpose of producing agreement.*
   Intercession focuses on the needs of others. This is powerful praying. When we pray for someone else's needs to be met we are acting in Christ's stead! The enemy attempts to hinder us from interceding through a lack of emotion or interest in another's needs. When we are unconcerned about the needs of others we cannot fully intercede for them as Christ would have us to.
   Our intercession is vital to the Kingdom of God. Without it many souls will continue to struggle and sin will continue to rule. We cannot just look at issues people face and respond with "That's a shame!" We must intercede!!! With intercession needs can be met and God can be glorified. Lives can be changed, souls can be saved, healed, delivered and marriages can be restored.
   These are issues the enemy battles us over - especially souls. God needs you to pray with importunity for people everywhere. Are you available? He will prompt you at certain times to intercede for others. You may not know the reason why - just be obedient to His Spirit and intercede.

Notes:

Day 25   Wait on the Lord   Psalms 27:13-14

I had fainted, unless I had believed to see the goodness of the LORD in the land of the living. 14 Wait on the LORD: be of good courage, and he shall strengthen thine heart: wait, I say, on the LORD.

    This word *wait* means to *expect, to bind together by twisting, to be joined to.* There are times when we must wait on God before receiving the blessings God has for us.

    It is in waiting for the manifestation of an answer to prayer that we have to wade through the difficulty of delay and/or discouragement. We find in verse thirteen that David would have fainted or given up hope had he not believed to see the goodness of the Lord in the land of the living. David expected to receive his answer while on earth not in the sweet by and by. After David received his answer he could give the encouragement for us to wait on the Lord and be of good courage.

    Don't give up on God even when you have to wait for an answer. Waiting is an attitude of the heart before God. It is an act of faith. It is active not passive. Waiting on the Lord does not mean that we sit idly by and do nothing. We must continue to trust God, delight in the Word, walk in obedience and have fellowship with God. When you go to a restaurant your waiter asks you *"How may I help you?"* or *"Can I get anything for you - what would you like?"* This is also how we wait on the Lord.

    We must ask Him, *"Lord, how may I serve You? What would You like for me to do?"* As we walk in obedience to the Lord's instructions we become joined to Him in our spirit. In the midst of waiting, trusting, and delighting in the Word the Holy Spirit will do a new thing within us. He will give us new strength and new revelation. We must believe to see the answer that God has promised. Don't give up on God. *Wait on the Lord: be of good courage, and He will strengthen your heart!*

Notes:

Day 26   Don't Faint   Luke 18:1

And he spake a parable unto them to this end, that men ought always to pray, and not to faint...

To faint means *to lose heart.* Doubt, fear, unbelief, and discouragement cause us to faint. We must be careful to guard against these when prayer is not answered immediately or life isn't going the way we want. As we read verses two through eight in this scripture, we find that this widow received her request because she kept asking.

She did not faint and give up. God honors and rewards persistent faith in prayer. An immature pray-er will give up and sink into not praying at all when the prayer is not answered immediately. A mature prayer will be consistent and persistent knowing that sometimes it is a spiritual battle to engage in prayer.

As we read further in Luke 18, we find that the Lord gives more parables concerning prayer. Jesus taught with the intent of saving us from faintheartedness and weakness in praying. Persistence requires patience and courage that will not waver. We read in Matthew 9:27-30 of the blind men who followed Jesus through the streets. They continued to follow Jesus into the house.

With persistence in following Jesus they finally received their request - their sight. Their persistence won where halfhearted indifference would have failed. Faith and persistence are inter-related. Our praying must be done with an energy that will neither tire or retire! We must not faint!

Notes:

Day 27 — Targets of the enemy — Ephesians 6:12-13

For we wrestle not against flesh and blood, but against principalities, against powers, against the rulers of the darkness of this world, against spiritual wickedness in high places 13 Wherefore take unto you the whole armour of God, that ye may be able to withstand in the evil day, and having done all, to stand.

Because so much can be obtained through prayer: salvation, healing, deliverance and restoration, the enemy of our souls will not allow us to pray without a fight.

Wrestling is an up close encounter with another individual. When we wrestle with the enemy it is an up close encounter. The enemy of our souls tries to get in our space, in our face, and in our thoughts. If the enemy can get you thinking his thoughts he can get you acting his ways and believing his lies.

Why all this fighting and conflict? Being a Christian has made you a target of the enemy. The enemy of our soul is still trying to thwart the purposes and plans of God. We are subject to troubles, perplexities, and persecutions even as Jesus Christ was when He walked on earth as the Word made flesh. Jesus Christ is still being subjected to these things on earth through Christians. We are earthen vessels who carry "Him" on the inside. This is why the devil fights against the believer so hard. We are Christians - Christlike, anointed by God. And you thought it was just about you!? No, my friend, the warfare is because of Christ in you!

The devil is still trying to attack and destroy Christ – the anointed one - so he attacks Christians who carry the anointing. As Christians, the presence of Christ dwells within us - this is what makes us targets of the enemy.

It is our presence as the salt of the earth; a light that cannot be hid that the enemy is intent on eliminating from the earth. The Holy Spirit, the Word of God, and the love of God within the believer is the mark that the adversary looks for. For this reason we must put on the armor of God and remain prayerful and obedient to the Word of God.

Notes:

Day 28   **Fast and Pray**   Matthew 6:16-18

Moreover when ye fast, be not, as the hypocrites, of a sad countenance: for they disfigure their faces, that they may appear unto men to fast. Verily I say unto you, They have their reward. 17 But thou, when thou fastest, anoint thine head, and wash thy face; 18 That thou appear not unto men to fast, but unto thy Father which is in secret: and thy Father, which seeth in secret, shall reward thee openly.

    The word *fast* in this scripture means *to abstain from food.* It is no wonder that food should be fasted because this is what caused the fall of man. Adam and Eve were disobedient to God in eating what they were told not to eat.

    A great hindrance to hearing and discerning the voice of God is our inability to remain focused on God's eternal Word because of our appetite that cries out constantly. When we choose to fast from food or anything that controls our physical senses, the Spirit of God sharpens our spiritual discernment. Fasting helps to clear our mind and heighten our spiritual awareness so that we can focus better on the things of God. Just as eating physical food strengthens our physical life, fasting strengthens our spiritual life. It humbles our soul before God and puts appetites under submission to the Holy Spirit.

    The motives and purposes for a fast should be Christ-centered. It is not to hurry God or hold God hostage like a child who holds his/her breath. It is not to force God's hand. Fasting helps us to deny self so that we may come in line with God's Word. Fasting is done to give God our full attention. In fasting we are saying, *"Lord you are more important than anything else. I desire to be more yielded to Your Spirit."* Combined with prayer, fasting helps us to focus on the Word of God more clearly. It helps our heart to receive clear direction from God.

    Although there aren't any set rules given as to how long or how often it should be done, Jesus expected His followers to fast. Bible fasts have lasted from one to forty days. If you are new to fasting, start with missing one meal a day. Use that time to pray and to read the Word of God. As you master one meal then progress to two, then a whole day. It will take discipline - but it can be accomplished. If you take medicine consult with your doctor first.

Notes:

Day 29 Trust in the Lord with all your Heart Proverbs 3:5

Trust in the LORD with all thine heart; and lean not unto thine own understanding

This word *trust* in the Hebrew is *batach*. Batach means *to attach oneself to; to be confident; be secure*. We trust God by attaching ourselves to His Word. This builds confidence in the Lord that He is able to fulfill His promises. A few years ago when the tsunami hit it was a most horrific scene to watch on TV. Several days after the tsunami we started seeing televised reports of people who had actually survived this terrible ordeal. They survived because they had attached themselves to something stronger than they were. Many people survived because they were in coconut trees and clung to the branches.

Some had to hold on for more than 20 hours before they were rescued. Through the storm and being overwhelmed with the waves of water and debris they held on for dear life. This is how we can *batach* or trust God. We will find our security and strength in Someone stronger than the situations we face in life. We must hold on to the Word of God for dear life.

Ecclesiastes 3:1 tells us *To everything there is a season, and a time to every purpose under the heaven...* Yes there will be seasons of trials and tribulations, storms will continue to rage in our lives but we must continue to stay anchored in the Word of the Lord! Whatever season we experience we must trust in the faithfulness of God.

In John 14:18 Jesus tells us *I will not leave you comfortless: I will come to you.* The Holy Spirit who is our constant companion will lead and guide us into all truth. The Word of God is truth. The Holy Spirit will guide us into trusting the Word so that we won't lean to our own reasoning or understanding.

Notes:

Day 30 — The Power of Agreement — Matthew 18:19-20

Again I say unto you, That if two of you shall agree on earth as touching any thing that they shall ask, it shall be done for them of my Father which is in heaven. 20 For where two or three are gathered together in my name, there am I in the midst of them.

The word *touch* in this scripture is *sumpatheo*. It means *to be compassionate with; demonstrates a connection with; to affect with some feeling or emotion, especially tenderness, sensitivity, or understanding.*

The word *agree* in this scripture is *sumphoneo*. The word *sumphoneo* means *to sound together, to be in accord, or in harmony with.* We get our English word *symphony* from this Greek word.

The power of agreement in prayer between two or more believers has much authority. As Christians, we are not just members of one family called the local church. We are members of a much larger family called the Body of Christ. We depend on and need one another.

God does not want us to always pray alone. He desires that we partner with other believers in the Body of Christ. There are times when we need to be alone with God and pray and seek His face, however, there is great spiritual power that is released when Christians have a spiritual symphony of agreement in prayer.

It is not enough to have a mental agreement in general about anything someone may ask. What is prayed for must first be in line with God's Word, and be a matter of united desire and harmony. Our hearts must be touched by the things that touch the heart of God. The extent to which the Holy Spirit can freely move within our lives, Church family, the Body of Christ, and into a dying world has a lot to do with the union, agreement, and obedience of the Christian.

It is especially important that husbands and wives exercise the power of agreement in praying together. When you agree in prayer over your marriage, family matters, finances, children, and anything else, God will be in the midst of your praying.

Notes:

Other Books by Patty Harris

Blessed are They that Mourn
Bible- Find - A - Word Puzzles (Vols. I-VII)
Comforting Those who Grieve
Conquering Holiday Grief
Fear Nots for Everyday (Series)
Fear Nots for Those who Grieve
God Has An APP for That!
Pray-er Points to Ponder
PrayerWalking!
Praying in the Key of "C"
Restoring the Gates of Prayer
Surviving the Death of a Loved One
The T.A.S.K.S. of the Pray-er
The Truth about Strongholds
What You Can't Lose in the Midst of Loss

www.ingramcontent.com/pod-product-compliance
Lightning Source LLC
Chambersburg PA
CBHW020022050426
42450CB00005B/598